Brief Family History and Genealogy

EDRIS KIBALAMA

Copyright © 2021 Edris Kibalama

All rights reserved.

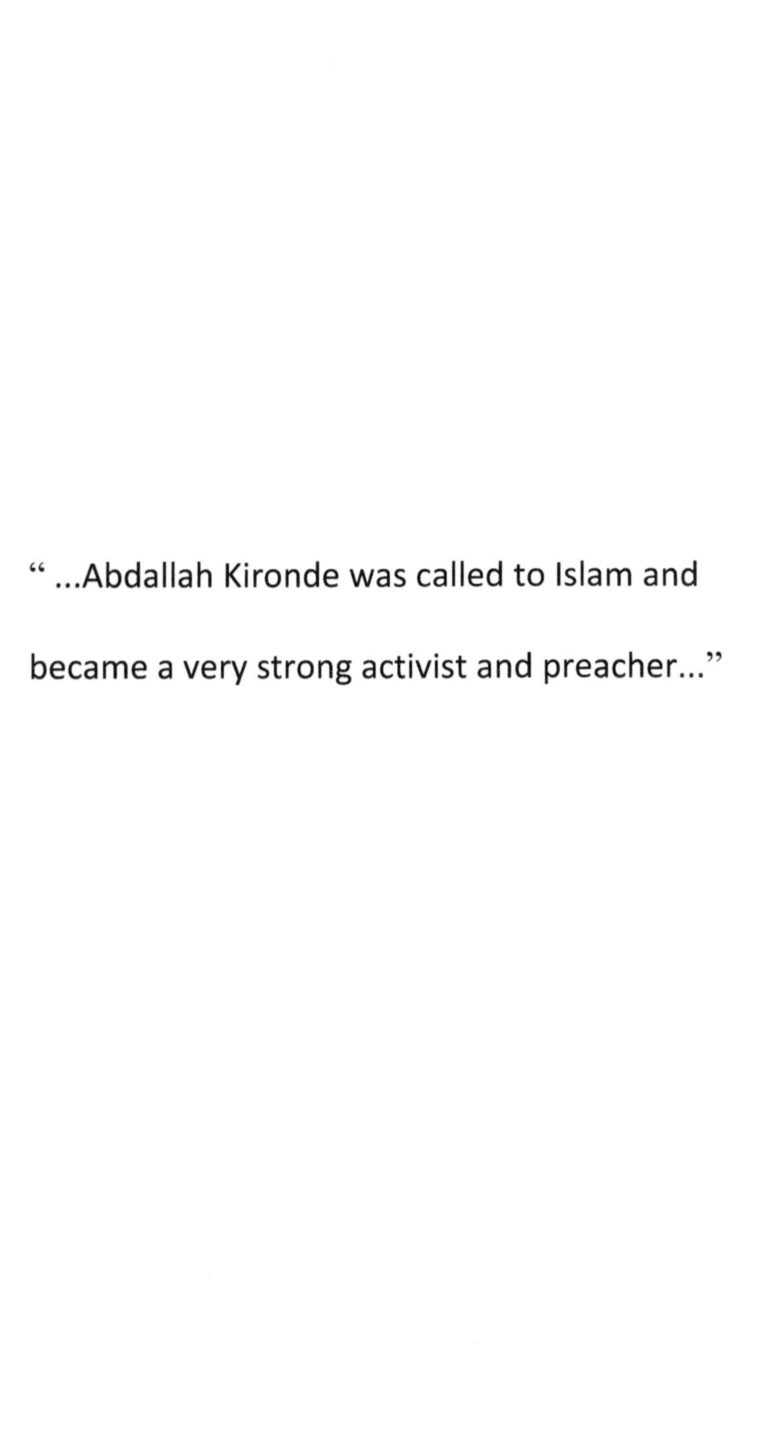

" ...Abdallah Kironde was called to Islam and

became a very strong activist and preacher..."

Table of Contents

INTRODUCTION

Bismillah Arrahman Arraheem

In the name of Allah, The Entirely Merciful,

The Especially Merciful

Alhamdulillah/All praise be to Allah

The Salah and salaam on the Final Messenger

of Allah(Muhammad peace of Allah be upon

him)

To proceed:

" ...Abdallah Kironde was called to Islam and became a very strong activist and preacher..."

This is a book that I compiled from a deep love to share many of the spiritual gems and treasures which I have come across thus far in my continuing Journey, until we reach physical death, then The life of the grave, then Judgement day and its many events, then to either Heaven/ Paradise, or to Hellfire. May Allah guide us Ameen. May Allah give us the good of this life, the good of the next, and May He protect us us from the punishment of Hellfire Ameen.

May Allah guide us all Ameen

May Allah forgive me my sins and May He pardon my mistakes

Alhamdulillah/All praise be to Allah. And the Salah and salaam on the Final Messenger of Allah(Muhammad peace of Allah be upon him)

Edris Kibalama

Jumada Awwal 1443 AH

THE TEXT

ABUDALLAH KIRONDE

Jaaja 'Abdallah Kironde used to live in Butambala, Kibibi, where he was initially burried, then his body was moved to Kyabadaza Butambala.

Jaaja 'Abdallah Kironde's elder children were of the same mother: First the late Musa Musoke, then President Yusuf Kironde Lule, then the sisters the late Nalongo and Hajat Balimutajjo), then Ibrahim Kabanda(youngest)

Please note that some of the late great grandfather Kironde's children were given names from the Mbogo clan. This was due to a family misunderstanding when Abdallah Kironde was called to Islam and became a very strong activist and preacher. His father Ntwatwa Semwaka was a Christian and given the circumstances it must have been very unheard of. Possibly Abdallah Kironde spent some years denounced from the Nkima clan so he lived with his Mum's side and hence the children born during this unsettlement were named Mbogo names.

Other children included the late Hajat Sarah Nabanja married to the late Kabanda (Bugirita

– prominent Nick name due to his successful business in Razor Blades)

Hajat Aidah who lived and built her house in Kasubi near the Kabaka tombs.

Mr Kamulegeya who used to live in the surburbs of Mulago hospital and was a teacher at Kololo Secondary School. And a few others.

Kibalama was a brother/ cousin to 'Abdallah Kironde. He was also religious in Islaam.

Kibalama lived in Bulemezi and Jaaja 'Abdallah Kironde lived in Kibibi Butambala.

PROFESSOR LULE IN OFFICE AS PRESIDENT OF UGANDA

History -

https://www.statehouse.go.ug/past-

presidents/president-yusuf-kironde-lule:

"

13 April 1979 to 20 June 1979

President Yusuf Kironde Lule

Yusuf Kironde Lule holds a record among all the eight Presidents of Uganda. He served he shortest time of just 68 days or two months and eight days.

Lule was born to Abdullah Kironde of Mpigi district in January 1912. His father sent him to a local primary school in Mpigi before joining the prestigious King's College Budo and later Makerere College to study education, with a specialty in Sociology. Lule was a very intelligent learner. He graduated top of his class and became a lecturer in the

department of Education at Makerere
College.

Lule later got several scholarships to study at
Fort Hare University, in South Africa and the
UK before coming back to Uganda to
continue working as a lecturer at Makerere
University. It was soon after his return from
studies that he was named the first black
principal in 1964.

In 1970, Obote removed him as Makerere
University vice-chancellor and replaced him
with Prof. Frank Kalimuzo. Lule went back to
the civil service after leaving Makerere. When

Obote was overthrown and pertaining to existing killings, Lule fled to exile just like many other Ugandans. He settled and worked in the UK, but kept in touch with fighting Amin.

To most observers, Lule played a mere side role in the fight against Idi Amin. Because of this, they thought that there was no way he could have become President. However, it was believed that most of the politicians, who came to attend the 'famous' Moshi Conference after the overthrow of Idi Amin, saw Lule as the cleanest of them all. He in fact had not even come for the meeting. He was then hastily invited for the conference and subsequently, he was named the President.

A ministerial system of administration was adopted and a quasi-parliament - the National Consultative Commission (NCC) was created. The NCC and the Lule cabinet reflected widely differing political views.

Having virtually 'boarded' the liberation train at its tail end made Lule merely a puppet of various other forces. Unfortunately, Lule did not even know he had very limited powers. The real power lay in the hands of Nyerere and Paulo Muwanga, who was preparing the return of Dr. Milton Obote, and the UNLF cohorts. So, in trying to assert his authority as president, little did Lule know he was committing a grave mistake.

His plans to reform recruitment into the armed forces; was seen as undermining the army. It was also viewed as a threat to the dominance of the so-called traditional areas for army recruits such as Acholi and Lango. Lule's proposal to disband the National Liberation Army to replace it with a newly-created National Army was viewed as a malicious move to sideline those who formed the bulk of the liberation force-including Generals like David Oyite Ojok.

On June 20, 1979, the NCC staged a coup, removing Lule as president for allegedly making wide ranging appointments in government without consulting them. Subsequently, Godfrey Binaisa was named as his successor.

Out of office, Lule went to exile in Tanzania, where he was put under house arrest by Nyerere. He suffered ill health and his doctor pleaded with Nyerere to have him released for treatment.

He was allowed to travel to the UK for treatment. But on improvement, he formed the Uganda Freedom Fighters (UFF) that later merged with Yoweri Museveni's Popular Resistance Army (PRA) in 1981, to form the NRM with Lule as president and Museveni as vice.

In 1984 however, Lule fell ill and died of kidney failure at Hammersmith Hospital in London. Museveni then took over and steered a five-year guerilla war, capturing power on January 26, 1986. Lule was given a state funeral and declared a national hero after the NRA captured power in 1986. Later, one of his sons Wasswa Lule became Member of Parliament for Rubaga North."

During 2 months of Presidency of Professor Yusuf Kironde Lule, my Dad was staying between Jaaja Kabanda's house in Kololo and The State house

Jaaja Kabanda was exiled to Nairobi. Professor Lule was exiled to Tanzania. They both had British ties. Professor Lule died in the UK. His body was returned to Uganda and burried at Kololo Air strips and a road nearby was named Yusuf Lule Road after his name.

EDRIS KIBALAMA

My Village in Uganda: Kyabadaaza

Butaambala

My father – The late Ishaka Kikabi Kironde

Ssali lived at Kawempe

My immediate grandfather Omugenzi Musa

Musoke eyebase Kyabadaaza Butambala,

Masaka Road.

Great grandfather Abdallah Kironde His

village was in Kibibi village, Butambala,

Great great grandfather - Ntwatwa

Semwaaka (He was a Christian).

FINAL PRAYER

May Allah increase us in beneficial knowledge. May Allah guide us, May Allah forgive us all our sins, and we ask Allah that he pardons us our shortcomings. May Allah purify our hearts and intentions, May Allah give us understanding of the religion, May Allah give us beneficial knowledge, hikmah and sincerity for His sake Alone. May Allah have Mercy and forgiveness upon us and those who preceded us.

Oh Allah guide us all Ameen

Rabbanaa, Aatinaa fiddunia hasanah, wa fil akhirati hasanah, wa qinaa 'adhabannaar

Alhamdulillah, wassalatu wassalaam 'alaa Rasuulillah

Our Lord/ Rabb, Give us the good of this world and give us the good of the afterlife and protect us from the fire of Hell Ameen

All Praises abundant and plentiful belong to Allah, and peace be upon his final Messenger Muhammad, peace and blessings be upon him, his family, his companions and all of those that follow them till the day of Judgement.

FINAL WORD

If you liked the reflective quotes, check out in the links below what was part of the fruits of this work:

1. www.edriskibalama.com

A website on creatively designed inspirational quotes images and a portfolio section outlining my achievements thus far.

2. www.muslimhomeschoolsoftware.com

A website on Home Educational Software for children with an Islamised and Ethical curriculum

3. www.intelligentmindsconsultancy.com

A website on IT support, WordPress support and IT consultancy

4. www.eddykibs.com

More of my inspirational quotes merchandise

5. To contact me and see my works:

www.linkedin.com/in/edriskibalama/

6. Other published books

Search: "Edris Kibalama" on

<u>www.amazon.co.uk</u>

Appendix

<u>Muziro (clan- genealogy)</u>

Nze bampita Edirisa Kibalama

Ndi Mutabani wa Ishaaq Kikabi Kironde Ssali,

Ndi muzukulu wa Musa Musoke Ssekiziivu,

Muzukul wa 'Abdallah Kironde, abebase

Kyabadaza Butambala,

Muzukulu wa Ntwatwa Semwaaka ekibibi

Butambala,

Nsibuka ewa Mugema e'Bugema

Neddira Nkima

Musa Musoke muganda w'omugenzi

Professor Yusuf Lule, eyaliko President wa

Uganda mu (1979) Lukumi murwenda nsanvu

mumwenda

BONUS CHAPTER 1

Extracts taken from:

Reflections of an Orthodox Islamic Immigrant

1. Parable of the importance of knowledge:

Know your button mushroom from a magic

mushroom, as eating one is a blessing, and eating the other is a potential sin.

2. Parable on dedication: When the light refuses to switch on, use an alternative power supply.

3. Importance of travel: Sometimes, the things you wish for are not always in the locality you currently reside in.

4. Tests of Allah: It is not until you live deeply amongst the ignorant , that you would know whether you are yourself the same.

5. In a land of deep seated Jahiliyyah, I give you an advice my fellow brother or sister, never open Pandora's box even if you can physically get out eventually, the spiritual, emotional and intellectual damage to your being may never heal.

Important lesson; Never argue with an ignorant one. Don't even contemplate or think about it.

6. Always turn back to the Creator. Don't let the people's negative, abusive and derogatory words put you down. Trust in Allah, He will

fulfill his promise to those who fear and trust
Him alone.

7. If you are following a path that you are not
meant to follow, the Creator will make it very
clear to you, as long as you constantly seek
His counsel. (i.e. Istikhaarah), you are sincere
and you demonstrate never-ending patience
(only for the sake of Allah)

BONUS CHAPTER 2

Statements on the reality of Orthodox Islamic Zuhd

1. Most poor people are not actually Zuhaad.

2. The richest man can be the greatest Zaahid than the poorest of people

3. Zuhd is a state of heart not necessarily a state of physical existence.

4. If most people knew the status of a true Zaahid (i.e. those that died in the pleasure of

Allah) no one on this earth would dare to even utter a word of negativity towards them, and moreover their Creator.

5. The Zuhaad are amongst the ones that Allah chooses to be from amongst His Awliyaa and from amongst His Khaleel

6. You'd rather abuse a mushrik than even attempt to have bad intentions towards a khaleel/ walii/ sincere a'rifun/ Zaahid of Allah

7. All the Prophets were Zuhaad

BONUS CHAPTER 3

Short statement from a semi- fruitarian,

ethical living Advocate and a World change

proponent through self-rectifying Activism:

One fruit a day keeps the Doctor away,

Five fruits a day keeps the Physician at bay,

Ten fruits a day puts the Surgeon in disarray.

And adding plant based, whole grain foods,

alludes to the unethical, malady- inducing

entities of perpetrating Bio-medical and

Health- Endangering downplay

-Edris Kibalama

#semifruitarian #semivegan #flexitarian

#edriskibalama #plantbased #healthyeating

#healthyeatinghabits #Fruits #health

#healthyfood #healthiswealth

#healthylifestyle #changetheworld

#personalchange #smallchangesbigresults

#smallchanges #smallchangesbigimpact

#smallchangesmakeabigdifference

#socialchange #youarethechange #ethical

#ethicalliving #ethicallifestyle

#personalchange #SelfRectification

#selfactivism

www.ingramcontent.com/pod-product-compliance
Lightning Source LLC
Chambersburg PA
CBHW072330270726
48658CB00016B/2263